www.tredition.de

AF186476

© 2016 Sir Edward Jones & Mr. SparX

Illustration: Sir Edward Jones

Verlag: tredition GmbH, Hamburg

ISBN

Paperback   978-3-7345-3816-2

Hardcover   978-3-7345-3817-9

e-Book   978-3-7345-3818-6

Printed in Germany

Sir Edward Jones & Mr SparX

"CRASHCOURSE"
Criminalistic

Crime scene-analysis, Pathology, Forensic Science

Introduction

Dear readers,

Welcome to our crash course Criminalistic.

In the following chapters, we simply explain the forensics.
We are very happy that you have chosen our technical book, and we hope you have fun reading it.

Sir Edward Jones

Mr SparX

First, the scene is the starting point of any investigation. Is there another injured victim at the scene, it must get first aid.

Then comes the crime scene. Nothing must previously be changed or touched without gloves. The crime scene is cordoned off a large area. All possible exits, places or escape routes are examined perhaps the offender has indeed hidden nearby.

The elucidation of a murder case is handed over to the homicide, and the head of this department organizes the handling of the case. He also informs the prosecutor, and possibly also the press.

One does not always have to search for the perpetrators. If it is still at the scene, he will be arrested. By traces and clues, such as fingerprints, by questioning the suspects and witnesses of the sequence of events is reconstructed. Explains the offender and the offense he puts a confession, the police are on the case to the prosecutor.

If the offender is unknown, the investigation needs more run faster to find him as soon as possible. It is checked whether the location of the body is actually the site of the murder. And if something has been changed at the scene, that is whether about money, jewelry or important papers was stolen. If something is stolen, no one possible motive for the killing may well be. In addition, the search is also for the murder weapon.

The timing is indeed important, witnesses must be heard. Who discovered the body? The time of the crime is particularly important, if the offender has disappeared. So the police knows about what advantage the offender has.

Fingerprints are taken, and searched for additional evidence. Everything is recorded accurately in a crime scene report. The body is examined by specialists. Its clothes, position or whether it has traces of a struggle, or hair, fingerprints or blood of another person. After the initial investigation, the victim is carefully transported to the coroner. There is established for example, whether the victim has had alcohol, ist last meal and what it was, whether it had been taking a medication and so on.

Has a witness seen the perpetrator for sure and he can describe it accurately, a mug shot is made on the computer. Is the description exactly, an investigation may be initiated. It is given to the other services, as well as radio and television.

All other activities will continue at the same time. While the body is examined in forensic, the traces in the crime lab are analyzed, interviewed witnesses´ statements are compared and gradually establish a sequence of events is collected. Chemists, physicists, dentists, biologists, genetic engineers and computer experts - they all work together.

The CID officials must create a criminal profile. Did the perpetrator know the victim? Did he know the crime scene? Has he chosen it consciously? Was it male or female? Is the act in connection with other acts? If it is a repeat offender?

As for the perpetrator, a profile is created also for the victim. Had it enemies? Had the deceased difficulties at work or private, financial or personal?

All these facts are gathered. Were there fingerprints of the offender, they will be compared with those in the police file. Little can be done to determine if the fugitives is an already known criminal or not.

With all this information the possible perpetrators are increasingly encircled. At the end, all the evidence is merged. An offender can be determined by positive evidence.

Maybe a suspect also confessed because of the evidence. Does the police solve the case and it has a suspect who could be identified as perpetrator, the case goes back to the prosecutor. The fast closure of a murder depends as you can read above on an incredible number of things. It is certain that the police must always work very precisely, thus must not oversee traces or destroy some and secondly ensure that not an innocent is suddenly under suspicion of murder. Therefore detectives must constantly carry out their profession with tremendous care and utmost responsibility. One must not be guided by false leads or fixate on the wrong suspects. One must always keep the overview.

Chapter 1 – Crime scene-Analysis

This chapter describes how the crime scene and it's evidence is secured.

What you got to look for on a crime scene:

1. <u>Crime scene-lock up</u>

The crime scene has to be locked up to safe it and all the possible evidence on it. The chain of evidence must not be interrupted.

2. Crime scene-sketch

The sketch of the whole crimescene
has to be made, for a complete
reconstruction of the course of events,
as well as having a accurate overview
of the scene.

3. Photographs

As every crime scene is individual, of
course it has to be photografic
recorded. Mostly images allow
another point of view for the several
investigators, which are the Detectives
and the forensic scientists, who can

have a look at the case-file anytime.Of course there will be made exact images of the victim as well as of the evidences in special, mostly with a scale for exact size-relations, for example bullet casings.

4. <u>Securing of evindence</u>

This includes several parts:

4.1 Fingerprints, of course the ones of the victim for secure identification, and if possible of the offender.

4.2 Shoeprints, mostly them of the offender, for calculating the size and weight of him and of course the way he took along the crime scene.

4.3 Wheelprints, to identify the possible vehicle of the offender, the way it took to the crime scene.

4.4 Cloth and hair, as there is possible DNA to secure.

4.5 Projektiles, eventually the whole murder-weapon, whatever this weapon may be.

4.6 Securing vehicles, for taking more evidence, such as fingerprints, DNA, cloth, and documents.

4.7 Cigarettes and tissues, both of them are perfect possibilities for DNA securing

4.8 Cellphones, Smartphones, Laptops and Tablets, all of them can take place in reconstructing the last hours, days and weeks before the crime. Mostly somewhere on these digital devices are important leads for the investigators. Even deleted data can be reconstructed.

4.9 Camera-surveillance. As in these days most public places, shops and private property is monitored, it´s possible that somehow the offender can be found on one of these mostly digital devices. Unluckily the average recording is just 24-48hrs, so the investigators have to be fast in finding all of the camera-recordings. Of course the quality of the recordings is essential. The better the surveillance-equipment, the better the possibillities of scaling up images and camera-recordings.

4.10 Witnesses.With good luck, the investigators find eye-witnesses, which are still one of the most important parts of investigation, even after all today's digital surveillance. If someone has witnessed the offender or even the crime itself,

a possible drawing of the offender can be made and matched within databases, national and international, if the offender has been reported before. After all, offenders are mostly indentified via fingerprints or DNA.

4.11 Presence of the pathologist. He can set the time of death by liver temperature, but as every crime scene is different, this setting depends on the temperature of the environment, the circumstances of death and the whole crime scene itself, even the weather is important when the crime scene is open air. So the closing examination is made in the lab, including the stomach intake, the skin structure, shotwounds/knifestabs , eventual injection points, color of the lips and tongue which can be lead to poisoning evidence, and many more.

Chapter 2 – The Pathology

The pathologist puts his attention primary on the cause of death of the victim. This is made by the dissection.
At the dissection, the pathologist makes sure that his examination is made absolutely accurate and precise.
The examination is made in 2 steps, by examine the outer body and the dissection of the inner.

The Outer Viewing

The pathologist´s first step makes sure an apparently diagnosis.

This can show a man inducted event.
The accurate outer prescription of the

body which can play a huge role, will be
named now:

1. The color of livor mortis

2. The grade of rigor mortis

3. The size and weight

4. Possible older injuries

5. Shot or stab wounds

6. Tattoos

7. Scars

8. Pigment contents

9. Surgery scars

10. Hematomas

11. Haircolor

12. Eyecolor

13. Shape of face and nose

14. Shape of ears

15. Inner mouth

16. Viewing of clothes if available

17. Image documentation of the whole body

The Dissection

The 2nd big step of the pathologist makes it possible to view the organs especially one by one. At this point, every single organ gets analyzed properly by microspcope and other several scientific tools.

The forensics get an accurate analyzis of every single part of the body.

The inner view will appear in 3 steps:

1. The opening of the skull.

2. The openig of the upper torso.

3. The opening of the lower torso incl. stomach content

1.   1.1 The opening of the skull happens with an electric bone saw

following the crest of the skull. By that, the pathologist gets to the open brain to get samples for a further examination.

1.2 and 1.3 When the opening of the torso happens, it goes by 2 kinds of cuts. The Y-cut and the T-cut.
For the Y-cut, the line goes from both collarbones aslope to the breastbone. The alternative T-cut goes almost similar from shoulder to shoulder and down to the pubis.

The following points are essential for the dissection!

1. Examination of the head

Documentary of the hair, color, length and thickness. Specifics like torn out hair, bacterial cell cultures and / or parasites. Examination of skull skin for injuries or older wounds.
The eyes, shape of skin and ears are examinded accurate for dust and microspopic particles.

Description of the whole mouth-area , searching for anything unsual inside the mouth. Of course there´s also made a detintion-imprint, what´s essential for identifying the victim if necessary when fingerprints or ID-documents are not available. If there are dental plates, the victim can be identified out of them too.

2. Examination of the neck-area

Inspection of the neck for eventual injuries, ability of movement, choking-marks and other signs of man-induced event.

3. Examination of the torso

The inspection of the torso shall show the shape and condition of it, which can show off older injuries.

4. Examination of the abdominal wall

This shall show the ratio to the chest, older injuries, scars and eventually marks of older surgeries.

5. Genital and anal examination

5.1 Male

Inspection of the penis, scrotum and inner injuries or/and ulcers

5.2 Female

Inspection of the vagina and labia for injuries and foreign matters. If the victim has been sexual assaulted,

a swab is made for detecting sperm as it can show the DNA of the offender.

6. Inspection of the back

Searching for violence-event, scars, wounds, where also can be be made swabs for further examination in the lab.

7. Arms and legs

Search for broken bones, injuries and discoloration.

8. X-Ray

An essential part of the dissection for making injuries of the scelleton

obvious which are not
to detect by eye or touching.

9. Removal of the organs

For an accurate dissection the
examination of the organs is one of
the most important parts.
If there´s something not clearly to see
for the pathologist, he will send the
organs to the forensic lab, where they
will be examined by microscope.
In the end of all that , the final
documentary of the dissection will be
given to the investigators.

Chapter 3 – Forensic Science

The forensic science includes 12 groups of analysis.

1. Forensic toxicology and serology

The toxicology shows eventually poisoning, drugs , pharmaceuticals and alcohol in the victim´s body.

Within the serology, bloodstains, DNA and other secretions are examined.

2. Forensic ballistics

The examination of fire-arms, projectiles,

stab-weapons and other items which could have been possibly used in an attack.

3. Fingerprint-identification

As the most offenders are identified yet by fingerprints, these will be checked on national and international databases.

4. Traumatology

The documentory of injuries.

5. Forensic entomology

This part checks the growth ratio of insects on the body.
By that one can tell for example how long a cadaver has been lying at a certain

environment, and the time of death can be detected.

6. Forensic phonology

This part comes up on blackmailing, when vicims get phone calls which are recorded by the police, or even data media which are mostly sended to the victims by the offender for orders.
Now the scientists can filter out noises, detect them for making the environment obvious where the media was recorded, and of course the blackmailer´s voice.

7. Forensic linguistics

It analyses blackmaling-letters by the form of writing or how sentences are built. By that , one can investigate the author.

8. Forensic dentistry

If a victim is not to identify the regular way, the forensics make dental print for making a comparison with eventually existing dentist´s files.

9. Forensic osteology

This means the identification through the skeleton.
If a victim has implants or artificial limbs, these have serial numbers. That numbers can lead to the victim´s identity.

10. Forensic psychatry

Here will be made an expertise about the offender. This is once important for the court, for the offender´s criminal responsibility, and second for the

offender´s grade of danger to the society.

11. IT-forensics

Within that, any electronic device will be searched for information.
This includes cell phones, personal computers, laptops, tablets and so on.
Mostly the investigators find here some proof of guilt , but also for the innocence of a suspect.

12. General forensics

This includes any kind of trace possible,

foot-prints, wheel-prints, ripping, break
marks on anything relevant, drilling
marks, oil- gas- or color marks.
All these will be put together for
assembling an accurate final result.

Chapter 4 – FAQ Of Criminalistics

1. How are bloodstains made visible after a crime scene was cleaned?

For this case, the forensics use a chemical liquid called Luminol
It reacts with the ferric particles in blood and makes it visible under black light. Unfortunately the chemic destroys the DNA structure in the blood, which makes the stains unuseable for DNA analysis.

2.How are fingerprints made visible?

Depending on the surface, fingerprints are made visible and can be taken by using several powders. Usually the powder will be put on the surface with a fine-haired brush and taken off the surface with a tape, which contains the print.

There are several powders in use, such as: Carbon black powder, iron-nitrate powder, iodine-powder, UV-powder, magnetic-powder and fluorescent powder . Of course there are powders that are only reacting in chemical way, such as: Malachite green, gentian violet, cyanacrylat and acetic acid.

At last I have to mention the X-ray, laser and stereoscopy.

3. What are faked traces?

Faked traces are these which are set on purpose to lead the investigators astray.

4.What is an indication?

Indications are not real proofs. They help
the court and the attorneys to find the
right way through the investigation.
An indication is as far as possible a fact.

5. What is a DNA-analysis?

Mostly a bloodstain, hair, skin-particles or
even a drop of sweat is enough to get
a genetic „fingerprint" These DNA-
patterns will be compared via national
and international data-bases to identify
the offender.

6. How are tire- and shoe-marks getting secured?

These kind of marks on the ground and other soft surfaces are taken by a plaster cast.
Most tires belong to cetrain cars and can be compared in data bases to ensure the car whcih has left the mark.

It´s kind of similar with shoe traces.
Every shoeprint is individual and can be related to his owner, if the shoe can be ensured.
Additional comes that shoes can include DNA traces as well.

7. What is a document-technique?

This is the chemical and physical investigation of any kind of document and certificate.

8. What is chemical analystics?

The analysis of several materials, little traces and particle mostly by mass spectrometer.

9. What is biological analystics?

That contains mostly ground analysis, cloth and any other presenting particle with biological origin.

10. What is a 3D-stripe light scanner?

This device captures shapes including traces without destroying the structure It gives a full 3D image.

11. How many kinds of traces exist?

There are 8 kinds of traces to separate:

11.1. Shape traces

11.2.Material traces

11.3. Situation traces

11.4. Fingerprint identification

11.5. Item traces

Traces which are made by machines, tools and any other object on severals surfaces.

11.6. Fake traces

11.7. Deception traces

Traces which are placed without purposal, meant to confuse the forensics.

11.8.Fitting traces

Broken parts, like glass , plastic, ceramic etc, which are recontructed by trial and error.

12. How does hair help the investigation?

It can be watched by microscope to get the color, structure and lenght.

13. How is a mug shot made?

This depends on eye-witnesses if available. The witness comes together with the police´s artists to describe what he/she has seen, meaning height, sex, face and bodyshape , color of hair and skin, shape of eyes, nose, mouth and even ears. The artist puts all this info together in a sepcial computer program that mostly gives a good result of an image of the suspect. If it´s done accurate, it even can be compared face-detection in surveillance-cameras.

14. How is the point of death determined?

Usually, as mentioned before, it´s done by checking the liver-temperature.

It also can be checked in the bowel. The temperature lowers about 1 degree celsius per hour, depending on the environment where the body has been found. The livor mortis give as well informations about the point of death. The forthcoming of the decay is also informative as well as the appearance of insects.This part ist done by the earlier mentioned entomology.

15. Wich parts are coming together in criminalistics?

Here we have: physicians, dental technicians, genetical technicians, biologists, pathologists, chemists, ballistic technicians, computer and network specialists and of course the investigating athorities.

16. What is questioned for assembling an offender´s profile?

Is the victim chosen intentional?
What is the background of his act?
Was it just a robbery gone wrong?
Is the deed in connection with other criminal acts?

Is the offender a recidivist?

Was the victim at the wrong place at the wrong time?
Did the offender know the crime scene before?
Did an escape plan exist?
Was the offender a hitman?
Is the offender eventually menatlly ill? Of course there´s made a victim´s profile as well.
Had the victim trouble or enemies?
Was the victim in debt?

Was the victim witnessing a crime and had to die cause of that?
All these are justified questions to close the case, which is surely hard to work out, but with all nowadays´ techniques and helpful methods it´s surely not as hard as in the past.

17, What is an alibi?

An alibi is most of all a proof of absence of a crime scene, but in most cases it´s a proof of innocence .
This can be ensured with camera images or testimonies.
Of course testimonies can be false, given by friends or family members.
If the authorities find out that´s the case, the witnesses can be set under prosecution.

18. What kind of crimes do exists?

Generally there are too many kinds to tell cause of the diversity of acts.
But one can say there are some fundamentals.

18.1 The crime:

This includes murder, man-slaughter, rape, sexual assault, bodily injury (with fatal consequences if one dies)

18.2 The offense
This includes theft, libel, insult of the dead, careless bodily harm, in some cases even sexual offense/assault on a ward.

18.3 Activity crimes

Such as false testimony, coitus inbetween blood-relatives

18.4 Endangerment

Here we have to separate sometimes in „normal" endangerment and abstract endangerment
In any case these include abandonment, arson, endangerment of traffic and environmental offense.

18.5 Permance crimes

Illegal restraint and breach of domestic peace

18.6 Special offenses
These include whistle-blow , crime in exalted position, corruption.

19. How can DNA been taken from a burned body?

In that case the DNA can eventually be extracted from the spinal marrow.

20. How is ballistic gel made?
This consists of 80% water and 20% gelatine

21. Is it possible to take fingerprints from objects drowned in water?

Simple as that, NO, the structure of a fingerprint will get destroyed under water.

Chapter 5 – Structure of a criminalistic team

1. Director

The head of everything, he is the knotpoint inbetween the several authorities and
takes care of a smoothly work and communication inbetween them.

2. Office of the district attorney

That sets the criminal prosecution, helps under circumstances with the investigation and is in responsibility under criminal law.

3 Investigative team-leader

He is responsable for that his investigators
are working according to instructions.
As a trained profiler , he surely
investigates by himself and puts the
results together.

4. The investigators

Such a team includes usually 4 -5
detectives, these take over several ways of
investigation. They share their
information on a regular basis and set
reports to the team- leader.

5 The pathologist.

He does the examinationof the victims
He´s one of the first in responsability on a

crime scene, he and the froensics ensure
evidence there and takes
care of the secure transport of the

body and found evidence to the lab.

6. The forensic team

That´s usually a team of 8
They work on molecular basis, examine
all the evidence which has been taken
together on a crimes scene.
Here are working all the stations together,
patholgist, dental technicians, biologists
and chemists.

7. The psychologist

He sets profiles of the offender as well as
of the victim. His expertise is an
important part of the investigation.

8. The IT-specialists

In that department work usually 2-3 pros on one case, they secure data from several devices and nowadays work out the mug-shot via special software.

9. Ballistics

That department examines weapons, shells, projectiles and even thrustings.

Chapter 6. - The Quiz At The End

1.What means ballistics?

_____

2.What are the violet spots on a dead body called?

_____

3.What is dactyloscopy?

_____

4.What examines the pathologist?

_____

5.How are blood staines on a whiped area made visible?

_____

6.How are tire- and shoe prints ensured?

_____

7.How is the temperature of a dead body taken?

_____

8.What is an alibi?

_____

9.How are images and videos taken?

_____

10. Where are fingerprints and DNA results stored?

_____

11.What's the name of the book?

_____

www.tredition.de

Dear readers

Thanks you for choosing the first book in this series. The next book will be published soon.

We hope you were able to read everything to your satisfaction well.

Regards

....

....

...

FSC
www.fsc.org
MIX
Papier | Fördert
gute Waldnutzung
FSC® C083411

Zeitfracht Medien GmbH
Ferdinand-Jühlke-Straße 7
99095 Erfurt, Deutschland
produktsicherheit@kolibri360.de